You Are a

GENIUS

at Something

201 IDEAS TO HELP YOU SHINE

DAISAKU IKEDA

World Tribune
Press

Published by
World Tribune Press
A division of the SGI-USA
606 Wilshire Blvd.
Santa Monica, CA 90401

Cover and interior design by *the*BookDesigners

24 23 22 21 20   1 2 3 4 5

ISBN: 978-1-944604-34-9
Library of Congress Control Number:
2019950128

CONTENTS

INTRODUCTION

We all want to be the best we can be, to be happy, to help others, to make a difference, to shine. We aspire. We hope. We make determinations. Along the way, we may come across an idea or bit of wisdom at just the right time to help us keep going through difficult times. Such a motto or phrase can determine the course of our lives.

"A human life is a succession of changes," Daisaku Ikeda writes. "What seemed changeless until yesterday may stand today at a fork in the road—beginning from this moment to change for the better or worse. What empower us amid this sea of change are guidelines that shed light on the correct path into the future and words of encouragement that revitalize us, especially in the midst of difficulty."

As the spiritual leader for millions around the world, Mr. Ikeda has spent his life helping people believe we can fulfill our dreams, we can overcome all adversity, we can do the good that only we can do, we are a genius at something. In essence, he has worked to spread the message that each person has the Buddha nature, the potential to lead a life of supreme good, happiness, courage, wisdom, and compassion that characterizes the life of a Buddha.

This philosophy is in many ways universal. People throughout the world and throughout the ages have offered many of the same lessons as Buddhism has. And Mr. Ikeda has searched out and shared many of these universal ideas.

In this collection, the editors have assembled 201 quotes we hope can become words to live by. About half come from Mr. Ikeda's writings and lectures. The other half are words he has shared with his readers and listeners over the decades. They are from writers, philosophers, activists, artists, scientists, Nobel Prize winners, and poets from nearly every continent and across centuries.

We arranged them into four thematic sections: Hopes and Dreams, Doing Good, Overcoming Adversity, and Building Character. Mr. Ikeda's quotes are unattributed on the pages that follow, while all the others have a name attached. For more information on these people, see the Profiles section starting on page 235 for brief bios.

Turn to any page, and our greatest hope would be if you find something that reminds you of what you need to do today or gives you a new perspective or makes you thankful for the life you have. A single quote won't change anyone's life in a day. But daily reflection on and application of the wisdom in these pages will definitely help you shine.

—The Editors

Hopes *and*
DREAMS

"TOO BIG" is just about the right size for young people's dreams.

JOSEI TODA

There is no true happiness for human beings other than chanting Nam-myoho-renge-kyo.

NICHIREN

If you think you can win, you can win. Faith is necessary for victory.

William Hazlitt

WHEN SERIOUS PRAYER AND HARD WORK COME TOGETHER, DREAMS BEGIN TO COME TRUE.

PRAYER FROM

CAN ACHI

NOTHING

IN THE

THE **HEART**
EVE WHAT
ELSE CAN
WORLD.

Mahatma Gandhi

There's something
about the written
what you want to
on the path to get

really magical
word. Writing down
do will put you
there.

LIFE IS
THE FOREMOST
OF ALL
TREASURES.

NICHIREN

I have discovered the secret that after climbing a great hill, one only finds that there are many more hills to climb.

Nelson Mandela

Keep moving forward

with a steady eye on the future,

telling yourselves:

"I'll start from today!"

"I'll start fresh from now,

from this moment!"

Wisdom emerges
through prayer.
Victory emerges
through wisdom.

Love your mission with a passion; there is nothing more beautiful.

AUGUSTE RODIN

WHO ANSWERS OUR PRAYERS? WE DO— THROUGH FAITH AND EFFORT. NO ONE DOES IT FOR US.

TRUST
THAT LITTLE THING IN
YOU THAT RESIDES IN
YOUR HEART.
MAHATMA GANDHI

THE INDIVIDUAL WRITES AND PERFORMS THE SCRIPT FOR HIS OR HER OWN LIFE. NEITHER CHANCE NOR A DIVINE BEING WRITES THE SCRIPT FOR US. WE WRITE IT, AND WE ARE THE ACTORS WHO PLAY IT.

If you can't fly then run, if you can't run then walk, if you can't walk then crawl, but whatever you do you have to keep moving forward.   MARTIN LUTHER KING JR.

PEACE

DOES NOT

EXIST SOMEWHERE

FAR AWAY. IT BEGINS

WITH OPENING

OUR

HEARTS.

THE

ONLY FAILURE

IS FAILING TO TRY.

ROSA

PARKS

I say try. If we never try,
we shall never succeed.

ABRAHAM LINCOLN

One day of life is more valuable than all the treasures of the universe.

Nichiren

YOUR

ENVIRONMENT

DOES

NOT

MATTER.

EVERYTHING

STARTS

WITH

YOU.

SEARCH

INSIDE YOURSELF

AND THERE

YOU WILL FIND ALL.

JOHANN WOLFGANG VON GOETHE

Follow the path you believe in, no matter what others think or do.

THE BEST PLACE FOR EACH IS WHERE HE STANDS.

HENRY DAVID THOREAU

Let where you
are going,
**NOT WHERE YOU
COME FROM,**
henceforth be
your honor.

FRIEDRICH NIETZSCHE

PRAYER

SUN OF

IS THE HOPE.

Nothing
great was ever
achieved without
enthusiasm.

RALPH WALDO EMERSON

WITHOUT YOU,
THE DOORS TO
A BRIGHT TOMORROW
CANNOT BE OPENED.
THAT IS WHY
YOU ARE SO VERY
IMPORTANT.

*The sun shines
and hope laughs
in the heart.*

PAUL CEZANNE

IF WE CANNOT
FEEL HOPE,
IT IS TIME TO
CREATE SOME.

LIFE

IS

PERPETUAL

CREATION.

RABINDRANATH TAGORE

A BEAUTIFUL PASSION EXPANDS THE SOUL.

GEORGE SAND

THERE'S
NO SUCH THING AS
ORDINARY
IN THE WORLD.
EVERYONE IS
EXTRAORDINARY.
AND EVERYONE CAN
DO SOMETHING.

BETTY WILLIAMS

RESOLVE TO BE THE SUN.

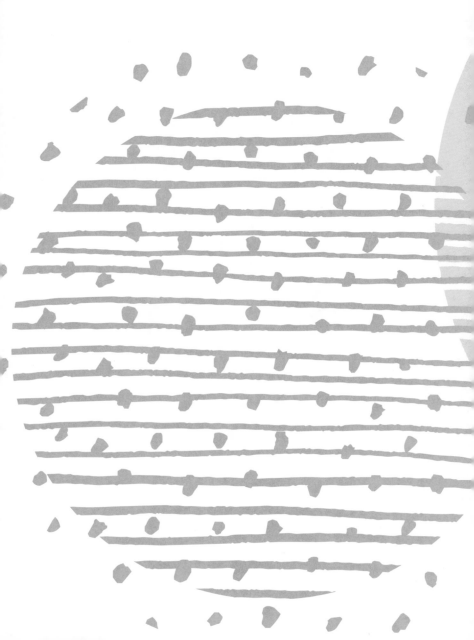

What is a road?
It comes of
trampling places
where no road
was before, of
opening up
wasteland where
only brambles
grew.

Lu Xun

A man's TRUE DELIGHT is to do the things he WAS MADE FOR.

Marcus Aurelius

The fact that we have been born into this world means that we each have a unique purpose to fulfill.

STRENGTHEN

YOUR

FAITH NOW

MORE THAN

EVER.

NICHIREN

Happiness is not in some far-off place. Happiness exists within your own life, within a single thought in your mind.

BELIEVE IN
YOUR OWN
LIFE! IT IS
THE SOURCE OF
UNSURPASSED
POWER!

*My first
step is to
create a
new person
of myself.*

Ahn Chang-ho

DO NOT BE AFRAID! LIVE OUT YOUR LIVES BOLDLY, AS TRUE LIONS!

Josei Toda

HENCEFORTH GOOD- I MYSELF GOOD-

I ASK NOT FORTUNE, AM FORTUNE.

Walt Whitman

To what use should we put our

we must continue to

lives? — this is a question

ask ourselves.

YOU ARE A GENIUS AT SOMETHING.

Keep a

rainbow of

hope in your

hearts.

THE

ANSWERS

TO YOUR

QUESTIONS

ARE

INSIDE

YOU.

EVEN IF
YOU TAKE A LONG,
ROUNDABOUT WAY TO GET
THERE, WHAT MATTERS IS THAT
YOU SUCCEED IN CROSSING
THE FINISH LINE IN
THE END.

It is the
heart that is
important.
Nichiren

You
were
born
to
win.

Doing
GOOD

When we change, the

world changes.

Kindness warms and courage cheers.

EMILY BRONTË

A sword is useless in the hands of
a coward.

NICHIREN

WHAT KINDS OF CAUSES AM I MAKING RIGHT NOW? WHAT ACTIONS AM I TAKING? THE ANSWERS TO THESE QUESTIONS ARE WHAT WILL DETERMINE THE **FUTURE.**

IF ONE LIGHTS A FIRE
FOR OTHERS, ONE WILL
BRIGHTEN ONE'S
OWN WAY.
NICHIREN

"HOPE

AND

KEEP

BUSY";

THAT'S

THE

MOTTO

FOR US.

LOUISA MAY ALCOTT

LET US GIVE
SOMETHING TO EACH
PERSON WE MEET:
JOY, COURAGE, HOPE,
ASSURANCE, PHILOSOPHY,
WISDOM, A VISION
FOR THE FUTURE.

> *Life's most persistent and urgent question is "What are you doing for others?"*
>
> **MARTIN LUTHER KING JR.**
>
>

Somewhere in the
world a mission is
waiting for you—
a mission only you
can fulfill.
It is waiting for you,
counting the days.

♥ ♥ ♥

The real test of my religion would be not how I treat the educated, but how I treat the man who can't write his name.

Benjamin Elijah Mays

If you devote your life
to helping others,
you'll stay young.

Seek to

person

be appre

100 gener

hence.

become a

who will

ciated

ations

Josei Toda

TO SERVE IS MY RELIGION.

MAHATMA GANDHI

FRIENDSHIP IS UP TO YOU, NOT THE OTHER PERSON. IT ALL DEPENDS ON YOU.

Instead of wor

whether you can

just go ahead

rying about

do something,

and try.

OUR LIVES SHINE WHEN TO BE OF OTH

BEGIN TO WE RESOLVE SERVICE TO ERS.

The PLEASURE OF the GREAT iS tO Make PeOPLe haPPy.

BLaiSe PaSCaL

IF HUMANITY COULD
ALWAYS REMEMBER THE
SPIRIT OF A MOTHER'S
LOVE, THERE WOULD BE
NO MORE WARS.

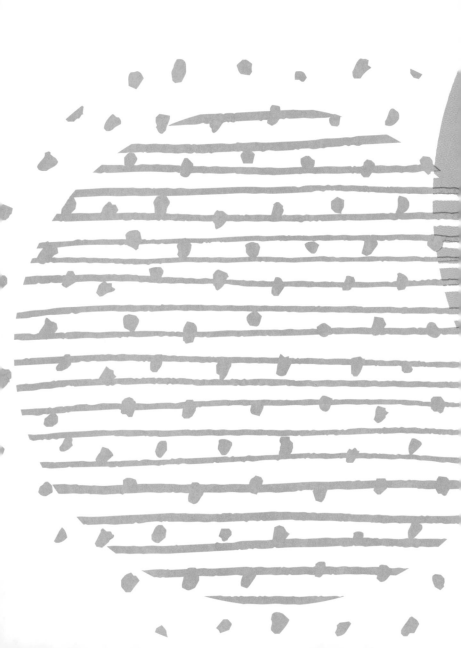

Thank you is a magic phrase that brings joy to both the person who says it and the person who hears it.

Whoever does not
help the right side is
helping the wrong.

John Stuart Mill

Only by defeating a powerful enemy can one prove one's real strength.

Nichiren

Faced with what is right,
to leave it undone
shows a lack of courage.

CONFUCIUS

All is joy,

when

fighting to

illuminate

the world.

JOSÉ MARTÍ

WE WILL NOT CHANGE THE HEARTS OF OTHER MEN BY MECHANICAL DEVICES; RATHER WE MUST CHANGE OUR OWN HEARTS AND SPEAK BRAVELY.

ALBERT EINSTEIN

Our attitude can change others' attitudes. If we change, those around us will change too.

I learned while fighting that my earthly duty is to disseminate happiness.

Pablo Neruda

ALWAYS AIM FOR
THE TOP,
WIN OVER YOURSELF,
AND CREATE A

PROUD

RECORD OF
TRIUMPH FOR ALL
THE WORLD TO SEE.

We live for
ourselves only
when we live
for others.

Leo Tolstoy

Those who now
believe in the
Lotus Sutra will
gather fortune from
ten thousand
miles away.

NICHIREN

A
SMILE
IS OFTEN
THE MOST
ESSENTIAL THING.
ONE IS REPAID BY
A SMILE. ONE IS
REWARDED BY A
SMILE.

ANTOINE DE
SAINT-EXUPÉRY

THOSE WHO CHERISH
A PLEDGE AND STRIVE TO
FULFILL IT ARE STRONG,
GENUINE, AND TRUE.

THE

BRAVER

ONE IS,

THE

HAPPIER

HE IS.

SENECA

I myself am
happiest and at
my best when
I am serving.

WANGARI MAATHAI

THE GREATEST
MEN ARE
ALWAYS
THE KINDEST.

STEFAN ZWEIG

MAKING ONE TRUE FRIEND IS A STEP TOWARD CREATING WORLD PEACE.

The greatest heroes are those who fight to help others, not those who fight for power and glory.
Ellen Key

One is a huge number. If you can help one individual, one child, you will then help ten.
Betty Williams

It is pleasant to be good—and it makes one strong and happy.

JOSÉ MARTÍ

"Joy" means

that oneself and

others

together

experience joy.

Nichiren

If we have even enough wisdom to distinguish hot from cold, we should seek out a good friend.   NICHIREN

DON'T SIT BACK AND COMPLAIN. WHO ARE YOU WAITING FOR TO TAKE ACTION? YOU MUST TAKE ACTION.

WANGARI MAATHAI

Overcoming
ADVERSITY

THE LION KING

FEARS NO

OTHER BEAST,

NOR DO

ITS CUBS.

NICHIREN

HAVING

LOTS OF

PROBLEMS IS A

GOOD THING;

IT'S WHAT

ENABLES

YOU TO

BECOME A

BUDDHA.

*Sweet
are the uses
of
adversity.*

♥ ♥ ♥

Shakespeare

Hope
is
courage.

♥ ♥ ♥

One could almost say
that the most excellent
among us derive
joy from suffering.

LUDWIG VAN BEETHOVEN

DIFFICULTIES
ARE BENEFITS.
BY CHALLENGING
AND OVERCOMING
THEM, WE CAN
FORGE A
CHARACTER
PURE AS GOLD.

IS IT A CALAMITY

BORN INTO FRESH

BLUSTERING TIMES?

GOOD FORTUNE?

TO HAVE BEEN
STORMY,
ISN'T IT YOUR

HERMANN HESSE

WINTER ALWAYS TURNS TO SPRING.

NICHIREN

REMEMBER THAT PATIENCE, IN AND OF ITSELF, IS A GREAT CHALLENGE, AND IT OFTEN HOLDS THE KEY TO BREAKING THROUGH A SEEMING IMPASSE.

If you summon

challenge some

never regret it.

your courage to

thing, you'll

COURAGE AND CHEERFULNESS WILL NOT ONLY CARRY YOU OVER THE ROUGH PLACES OF LIFE, BUT WILL ENABLE YOU TO BRING COMFORT AND HELP TO THE WEAK-HEARTED.

WILLIAM OSLER

Nothing guarantees our victory more than the heart of faith.

♥ ♥ ♥

i FiND DiFFiCULtieS eXCitiNG.

HaZeL HeNDeRSON

THOSE WHO CONTINUE TO CHALLENGE THEMSELVES IN THEIR OWN WAY, EVEN IF THEY LOSE SOMETIMES, WILL CERTAINLY FINISH AS CHAMPIONS.

NICHIREN'S DISCIPLES CANNOT ACCOMPLISH ANYTHING IF THEY ARE COWARDLY.

NICHIREN

Bravely overcoming one small fear gives you the courage to take on the next step.

Every struggle is a victory.

HELEN KELLER

The "sun" of self-confidence is certain to rise in the hearts of those who try.

DON'T RUN AWAY FROM YOUR PROBLEMS; FACE THEM!
Because if you don't deal with them, they will always be with you. Deal with a problem which arises; **FACE IT COURAGEOUSLY.**

NELSON MANDELA

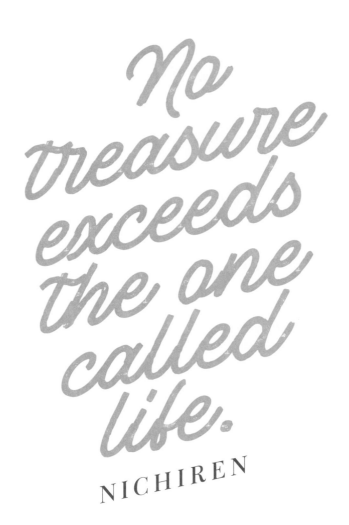

No treasure exceeds the one called life.

NICHIREN

I think it's important to have a good hard failure when you're young. . . . I learned a lot out of that.

Walt Disney

BEING **BORN IN A STATELY** MANSION IS **NO GUARANTEE** OF HAPPINESS, ANY MORE **THAN BEING** BORN IN A **SHACK DOOMS** ONE TO MISERY.

PUBLIC

SHOULD BE

NOT

OPINION MADE, FOLLOWED.

Elizabeth Blackwell

BY CHANGING THEIR WAY OF THINKING. PEOPLE CAN CHANGE THEIR LIVES.

The course of our lives is determined by how we react—what we decide and what we do—at the darkest of times.

To the weak, difficulty is a closed door. To the strong, however, it is a door waiting to be opened.

ALMAFUERTE

HAVING PROBLEMS AND WORRIES DOESN'T NECESSARILY MAKE YOU UNHAPPY, BUT BEING DEFEATED BY THEM DOES.

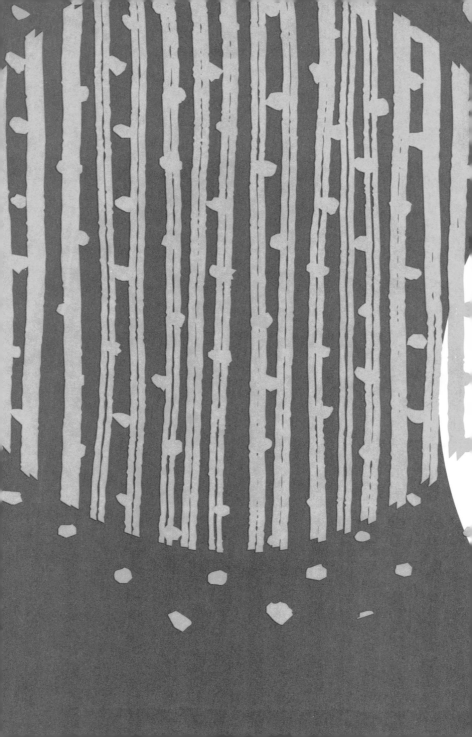

Those men are my enemies today, but tomorrow they may become my friends.

JOSÉ MARTÍ

The minute that passes doesn't matter to time, only the minute that's coming.
Joaquim Maria Machado de Assis

EVEN
THOUGH
YOU MAY BE
GOING THROUGH
A SAD OR DIFFICULT
TIME YOURSELF,
IF YOU TRY TO
ENCOURAGE
SOMEONE ELSE,
YOU WILL
FEEL
REFRESHED.

THE SECRET OF LIFE AND
CONTENT IS TO BEGIN A
NEW DAY WITH COURAGE
AND WITH THE BELIEF
THAT IT CAN BE MADE
THE BEST OF ALL DAYS,
WHATEVER CHANGE IT
BRINGS.

PEARL S. BUCK

The task that is without difficulty is almost without merit; there is great interest in triumphing over obstacles.

CHARLOTTE BRONTË

Think of the power that's in the universe—moving the earth, growing the trees. And that's the same power within you, if you'll only have courage—and the will to use it.
Charlie Chaplin

WE ARE POWERFUL AND TREMENDOUS IN OURSELVES.

WALT
WHITMAN

WE COULD NEVER LEARN TO BE BRAVE AND PATIENT, IF THERE WERE ONLY JOY IN THE WORLD.

HELEN KELLER

If you shine with radiant light, there can be no darkness in your life.

Resolve from the depths of your heart: "Now I will stand up and fight!" From that instant your destiny changes. Your life develops. History begins.

The important thing is not

that our resolve never wavers,

but that we don't get down on

ourselves or throw in the towel

when it does.

YOU MAY WRITE ME DOWN

IN HISTORY / WITH YOUR

BITTER, TWISTED LIES,

/ YOU MAY TROD ME IN THE

VERY DIRT / BUT STILL,

LIKE DUST, I'LL RISE.

MAYA ANGELOU

ONLY THOSE

WHO HAVE

EXPERIENCED

THE HARSHNESS OF

WINTER

CAN TRULY

KNOW

THE JOY OF

SPRING.

Riches, prestige,
everything can be lost.
But the happiness in your
own heart can only be
dimmed; it will always be
there, as long as you live,
to make you happy again.

♥ ♥ ♥

Anne Frank

Daring to take on tough challenges—that in itself is immense freedom.

♥ ♥ ♥

WHAT JOY IS, IS
ESSENTIALLY KNOWN
ONLY TO THOSE WHO HAVE
SUFFERED MUCH. OTHERS
KNOW ONLY PLEASURE,
WHICH IS IN NO WAY
SIMILAR.
CARL HILTY

A single brave individual can change the world.

THERE IS NO PARADISE. FIGHT AND LAUGH AND FEEL BITTER AND FEEL BLISS; AND FIGHT AGAIN. FIGHT, FIGHT. THAT IS LIFE.

D. H. LAWRENCE

WHERE THERE IS CHALLENGE, THERE IS **PROGRESS.** WHERE THERE IS **CHALLENGE,** THERE IS HOPE. WHERE THERE IS CHALLENGE, THERE IS JOY. WHERE THERE IS **CHALLENGE,** THERE IS **HAPPINESS.** WHERE THERE IS CHALLENGE, THERE IS **VICTORY.**

You have enemies?

of every man who has

created a new idea

why, it is the story

done a great deed or

Victor Hugo

BE BRAVE!

BE UNBEATABLE

AND SET OFF

PEACEFUL

IN SPIRIT.

TOWARD A

TOMORROW.

IF YOU'RE SAD AND
LONELY, THEN YOU SHOULD
ACKNOWLEDGE THOSE
FEELINGS. DON'T TRY TO
DISTRACT YOURSELF FROM
THEM WITH SHALLOW
AMUSEMENTS. DON'T
DIMINISH THEM. GO THROUGH
THOSE FEELINGS, BRAVELY
WEATHER THEM, AND TURN
THEM INTO NOURISHMENT
FOR YOUR

GROWTH.

THE IMPORTANT THING, ABOVE ALL, IS TO WIN OVER YOURSELF.

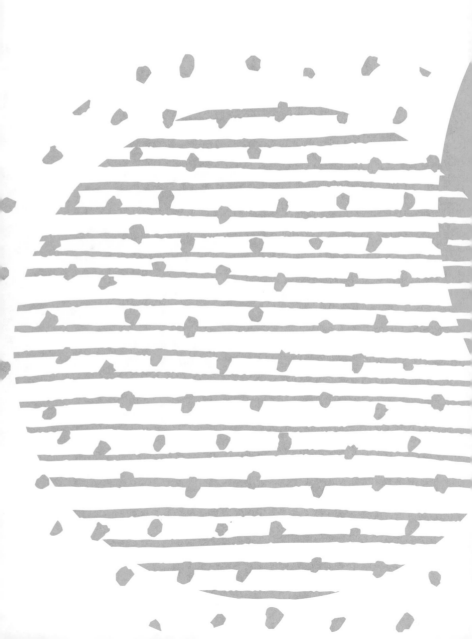

Nam-myoho-renge-kyo is like the roar of a lion. What *sickness* can therefore be an obstacle?

Nichiren

Building
CHARACTER

Nonviolence
is not a cover
for cowardice,
but it is the
supreme virtue
of the brave.

Mahatma Gandhi

Great people
never forget
what others have
done for them.

THE BEST WAY TO ATTAIN BUDDHAHOOD IS TO ENCOUNTER A GOOD FRIEND.

NICHIREN

Let us pick up our books and our pens. They are our most powerful weapons.

MALALA YOUSAFZAI

The more trouble, the more lion; that's my principle.

Ralph Waldo Emerson

THE ONLY REAL MISTAKE YOU CAN MAKE WHEN YOU ARE YOUNG IS GIVING UP ON YOURSELF.

LET'S LIVE
WITH A BIG
AND A BIG
SHINES
HAPPIEST WAY

OUR LIVES

HEART

SMILE THAT

IT IS THE

TO **LIVE.**

Effort is the

supreme joy.

PIERRE DE COUBERTIN

WHERE THERE IS
UNSEEN VIRTUE,
THERE WILL BE
VISIBLE REWARD.
NICHIREN

Without courage we cannot be compassionate.

♥ ♥ ♥

A

THOUSAND

SHEEP CANNOT HOLD

THEIR OWN AGAINST A

SINGLE LION.

TSUNESABURO
MAKIGUCHI

Instead of wanting to be like this or that, make yourself into a silent, immovable giant. That's what the mountain is.

EIJI YOSHIKAWA

> WHAT A WORLD OF
> DELIGHT LIES IN
> LEARNING.
>
> JOHANN WOLFGANG
> VON GOETHE

My mind,
I hope, is ever
growing, ever
moving forward.
Mahatma Gandhi

THE MAN WHO IS TO BE HAPPY WILL THEREFORE NEED VIRTUOUS FRIENDS.

ARISTOTLE

Courage is free.

Anyone can have it.

The important

thing is to

strive to win

where you are now.

To have the humility to learn something from anyone is a measure of how big a person is.

He who strives has already won.

JOSÉ MARTÍ

WILL YOU TAKE A STEP FORWARD, OR WILL YOU BE CONTENT TO STAY WHERE YOU ARE NOW? EVERYTHING IN YOUR LIFE IS DETERMINED BY THAT.

IT IS DARK,
BUT I SING
BECAUSE
TOMORROW
WILL COME.

AMADEU THIAGO
DE MELLO

Youth should not seek an easy, comfortable path.

IT IS OFTEN

THE PEOPLE WHO

REFUSE TO ASSUME ANY

RESPONSIBILITY WHO ARE

APT TO BE

THE SHARPEST

CRITICS OF

THOSE WHO DO.

ELEANOR ROOSEVELT

THE EASIEST

WAY TO BECOME

SAD IS

BY COMPLAINING.

GEORGE SAND

You cannot hope to build a better world without improving the individuals.

Marie Curie

There is no
one as strong
as a person
whose heart is
always filled
with gratitude.

♥ ♥ ♥

More than machinery we need humanity, more than cleverness we need kindness and gentleness.

CHARLIE CHAPLIN

WITHOUT CHEERFULNESS THERE IS NO STRENGTH.

TO DISCARD AND SEEK THE THE WAY OF COURAGE.

THE SHALLOW
PROFOUND IS
A PERSON OF

NICHIREN

To make an art of life!
That is the finest
art of all the
Fine Arts.
Florence Nightingale

START FROM THE PRESENT MOMENT. **BEGIN** SOMETHING, HERE AND NOW.

I still believe

everything, that

truly good

in spite of

people are

at heart.

Anne Frank

Challenge It doesn't what.

something.

matter

BUiLD YOUR happiNess through the happiNess OF Others.

VOLtaiRe

BOOKS INTRODUCE YOU TO THE
FRAGRANT FLOWERS OF LIFE, TO
RIVERS, ROADS, AND ADVENTURES.
YOU CAN FIND STARS AND LIGHT,
FEEL DELIGHT OR INDIGNATION. YOU
ARE SET ADRIFT ON A VAST SEA OF
EMOTION UPON A SHIP OF REASON,
MOVED BY THE INFINITE BREEZES
OF POETRY. DREAMS AND DRAMAS
EVOLVE. THE WHOLE WORLD
COMES ALIVE.

Talent . . .
is merely
long patience.
Keep on
working.

Gustave Flaubert

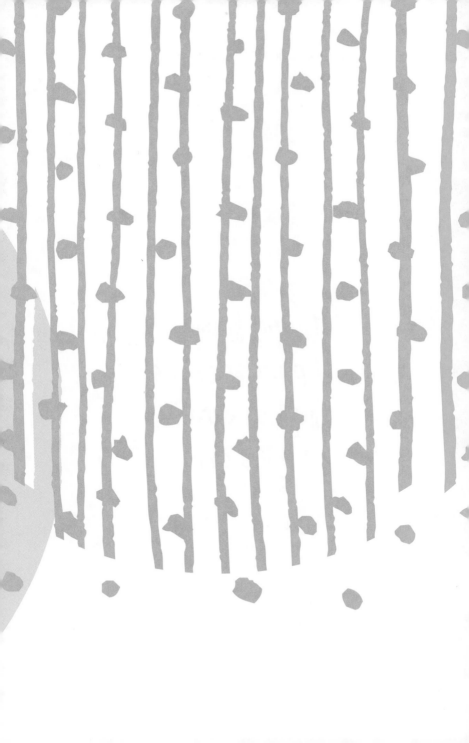

I long for work.
I pant for a life
full of striving.

W. E. B. Du Bois

The road
to self-
improvement
never ends.
There is
always room
to learn more,
to grow more.

THE MAN

WHO

STANDS

ALONE IS THE

STRONGEST.

HENRIK IBSEN

There is some good in every person if you can find it.

L. M. MONTGOMERY

YOU CAN'T REMAKE THE WORLD / WITHOUT REMAKING YOURSELF / EACH NEW ERA BEGINS WITHIN.

BEN OKRI

Every problem and worry you have now will help you build a solid, lasting foundation for your life.

Your true
rival is
yourself—
yesterday's self.

GIVEN THAT **STRUGGLES** AND CHALLENGES ARE AN UNAVOIDABLE PART OF **LIFE,** WE MIGHT AS WELL MAKE OUR WAY WITH A **JOYFUL,** POSITIVE **SPIRIT.**

TRUE VICTORS ARE
THOSE WHO KEEP ON
SMILING REGARDLESS
OF WHETHER THEY
WIN OR LOSE AND
MOVE ONTO THE
NEXT CHALLENGE
WITH EVEN STRONGER
DETERMINATION.

THE PLEASANTEST OF ALL DIVERSION IS TO SIT ALONE UNDER A LAMP, A BOOK SPREAD OUT BEFORE YOU, AND TO MAKE FRIENDS WITH PEOPLE OF A DISTANT PAST YOU HAVE NEVER KNOWN.

YOSHIDA KENKO

A truly smart person is someone who has lots of questions and continues asking *why.*

There's only a slight difference between thinking it's useless to even try and deciding to take on the challenge.

Josei Toda

Become the master of

your mind rather than

let your mind

master you.

Six Paramitas Sutra

WHERE THERE ARE
SMILING FACES
HOPE IS CREATED,
HAPPINESS
SPREADS, AND
PEACE SHINES.

OUR

ENVIRONMENT

DOESN'T DETERMINE

OUR HAPPINESS;

WE DO.

Good friends
gather around
those who strive to
learn and improve
themselves.

A noble life is one
dedicated to a noble vow.

My wish is that all my disciples make a great vow.

NICHIREN

THOSE AWAKENED TO THEIR MISSION ARE STRONG.

Have the guts
and integrity to
honestly admit your
errors.

Faith is—to fear nothing, to stand unswayed, the power to surmount any obstacle.

BE LAMPS

UNTO

YOURSELVES.

RELY ON

YOURSELVES.

SHAKYAMUNI BUDDHA

HATREDS DO NOT EVER

CEASE IN THIS WORLD

BY HATING, BUT BY

NOT HATING;

THIS IS AN

ETERNAL TRUTH.

THE DHAMMAPADA

*The treasures of
the heart are
the most
valuable of all.*

Nichiren

PROFILES of the
PEOPLE QUOTED

LOUISA MAY ALCOTT (11/29/1832–3/6/1888) was a best-selling novelist of the late 1800s, and many of her works, most notably *Little Women*, remain popular today. Her works, which featured strong, educated female heroines who challenged societal norms and sought their own individuality, greatly impacted American literature. (p. 66)

ALMAFUERTE (5/13/1854–2/28/1917), born Pedro Bonifacio Palacios, was an Argentine poet and educator, whose works often touched on the struggles of the poor and the oppressed. He was widely read among the working class and spoke out against society's treatment of the masses. (p. 136)

MAYA ANGELOU (4/4/1928–5/28/2014) was an American poet, memoirist, and civil rights activist best known for *I Know Why the Caged Bird Sings*, which tells her life up to age seventeen. The autobiography is now taught in colleges around the world. The quote is from her poem "Still I Rise." (p. 150)

ARISTOTLE (384–322 BCE) was a Greek philosopher and is considered one of the founders of Western philosophy. He wrote about many subjects, including physical science, metaphysics, ethics, poetry, music, economics, politics, psychology, and government, among others. His concepts are influential and much talked about even today. (p. 184)

MARCUS AURELIUS (4/26/121–3/17/180) was a Roman emperor from 161 to 180 and a philosopher of stoicism, the idea that virtue, especially self-control, is happiness. The quote comes from his most famous work, *Meditations*. (p. 40)

LUDWIG VAN BEETHOVEN (12/16/1770–3/26/1827) was a German composer and pianist, considered one of the greatest classical music composers of all time. Despite losing his hearing, he composed some of the most recognizable music in the world today, including his Symphony No. 9, the first by a major composer to use voices in a symphony. This symphony's finale features the "Ode to Joy," with its theme of universal brotherhood. (p. 112)

ELIZABETH BLACKWELL (2/3/1821–5/31/1910) was the first woman to receive a medical degree in the United States. A moral and social reformer, she was a pioneer in the education of women in medicine. She cofounded the London School of Medicine for Women, the first medical school in England to train women as doctors. (pp. 132–33)

CHARLOTTE BRONTË (4/21/1816–3/31/1855) was an English novelist and poet, elder sister to Emily and Anne, all three of whose novels became classics of English literature. *Jane Eyre,* her best-known work, revolutionized prose fiction by using first-person narrative to focus on the inner life of the protagonist. (p. 143)

EMILY BRONTË (7/30/1818–12/19/1848) was an English novelist and poet, best known for her only novel, *Wuthering Heights.* At first subject to harsh critical reviews, this passionate tale of love and hate is now considered a classic of English literature. (p. 62)

PEARL S. BUCK (6/26/1892–3/6/1973) was an American writer and novelist. She was raised in China by missionary parents, and her best-known novel, *The Good Earth*, about life in a Chinese village, won the Pulitzer Prize in 1932. She became the first woman to win the Nobel Prize in Literature, which was awarded for her "notable works which pave the way to a human sympathy passing over widely separated racial boundaries." In later years, Buck's humanitarian efforts supported a number of causes, including civil rights and the plight of Asian war children. (p. 142)

PAUL CEZANNE (1/19/1839–10/22/1906) was an influential French painter whose works helped form a bridge between the Impressionists of the late 1800s and the new art world of the twentieth century. (p. 32)

AHN CHANG-HO (11/9/1876–3/10/1938) was a Korean independence activist and early leader of the Korean American community in the United States. He was committed to reforming the character of the Korean people and Korea's entire social system. (p. 46)

CHARLIE CHAPLIN (4/16/1889–12/25/1977) was an English comic, actor, and filmmaker during the silent film era, some of whose films are considered among the greatest ever made, including *City Lights, Modern Times,* and *The Great Dictator.* His beloved character "The Tramp" became an icon for both his slapstick comedy and his struggles against adversity. When Hitler rose to power in the 1930s, Chaplin saw him as a villain and decided to fight against him and Nazism through his filmmaking, producing *The Great Dictator.* The film, which satirizes Hitler and condemns Nazism, became Chaplin's most commercially successful. The quotes are from *Limelight* and *The Great Dictator.* (pp. 144 and 196)

CONFUCIUS (551–479 BCE) was a Chinese philosopher whose humanistic ideas about kindness and self-cultivation have impacted people around the world and are still influential today. He was the first to use the so-called Golden Rule: "Do not do to others what you do not want done to you." (p. 86)

PIERRE DE COUBERTIN (1/1/1863–9/2/1937) was a French educator and historian and is known as the father of the modern Olympic Games. He idealized the ancient Olympic Games as a place for amateur athletes to compete and saw international athletic competition as a way to promote understanding across cultures, thereby lessening the dangers of war. (pp. 176–77)

MARIE CURIE (11/7/1867–7/4/1934) was a Polish and naturalized French physicist and chemist who pioneered research on radioactivity. Perhaps the most famous female scientist, she was the first woman to receive a Nobel Prize and the only person to receive two Nobel Prizes in two different scientific fields. (p. 194)

WALT DISNEY (12/5/1901–12/15/1966) was an American entrepreneur and film producer who was a pioneer in animation. He founded, with his brother, the Walt Disney Company, which has produced many of the most beloved and beautiful films of all time, including *Snow White and the Seven Dwarfs*, *Bambi*, *The Lion King*, *The Jungle Book*, and *Fantasia*. He won more Academy Awards than any other person, and his theme parks attract more than a hundred million visitors each year. (p. 130)

W. E. B. DU BOIS (2/23/1868–8/27/1963) was an American sociologist, historian, civil rights activist, and one of the cofounders of the National Association for the Advancement of Colored People. He was the first African American to earn his doctorate from Harvard and, through his many writings, spoke out against Jim Crow laws, lynching, and discrimination in education and employment. The quote is from his *The Souls of*

Black Folk, a cornerstone of African American literature and an important work in the history of sociology. (p. 210)

ALBERT EINSTEIN (3/14/1879–4/18/1955) was a German-born physicist whose theory of relativity, with its famous equation $E=mc^2$, forms the foundation for modern science. He won the Nobel Prize in Physics for his explanation of the photoelectric effect, which itself was key to the development of quantum physics. Though scientists used his theories to develop the atom bomb, Einstein advocated for peace and against militarism and nuclear weapons. (p. 88)

RALPH WALDO EMERSON (5/23/1803–4/27/1882) was an American essayist, lecturer, and philosopher who led the transcendentalist movement in the mid-1800s. Transcendentalism believes in the inherent goodness of people and nature and that people are at their best when they are truly "self-reliant." Among his best-known essays are "Self-Reliance," "The Over-Soul," and "Nature." The words on p. 172 come from what a poor woman once said to him. (pp. 30 and 172)

GUSTAVE FLAUBERT (12/12/1821–5/8/1880) was a French novelist, highly influential in bringing realism to fiction, especially in his masterpiece, *Madame Bovary*. The quote is from a letter he wrote to his protégé, the famed short story writer Guy de Maupassant. (pp. 208–9)

ANNE FRANK (6/12/1929–February 1945) was born in Germany, but her family moved to Amsterdam after the Nazis came to power in 1933. Germany occupied Holland in 1940, and in 1942 the family was forced into hiding in a "secret annex" in a building where her father had worked. For their two years in hiding, the thirteen-year-old Anne kept a diary, documenting the horrors of their life yet revealing the young girl's humanity and courage. The family was discovered and arrested in 1944, and only her father survived the concentration camps. He published the diary several years after the war, and Anne's message of hopefulness despite her tragedies makes the book a beloved work of literature still today. (pp. 152 and 202–3)

MAHATMA GANDHI (10/2/1869–1/30/1948) was the leader of India's independence movement and advocate of nonviolent, passive resistance. His teachings have influenced many civil rights advocates including Marin Luther King Jr. and Nelson Mandela. (pp. 6–7, 16, 74, 168, and 183)

JOHANN WOLFGANG VON GOETHE (8/28/1749–3/22/1832) was a German writer widely considered to be that country's finest and most influential literary figure. *The Sorrows of Young Werther*, his first novel, made him a celebrity. Other works, including *Faust*, inspired artists worldwide for decades to come. (pp. 24 and 182)

WILLIAM HAZLITT (4/10/1778–9/18/1830) was an English writer and social critic best known for his informal and humanistic essays on a variety of subjects. A contemporary of such literary giants as Coleridge, Wordsworth, and Keats, he is considered one of the greatest essayists in the English language. This quote comes from *Table Talk: Essays on Men and Manners*. (p. 4)

HAZEL HENDERSON (3/27/1933–) is a futurist, evolutionary economist, and a pioneer in the environmental and sustainability movement. She is founder of several initiatives to support and accelerate the transition to a green, ethical, and just economy. (p. 122)

HERMANN HESSE (7/2/1877–8/9/1962) was a German-born poet, novelist, and painter. He won the Nobel Prize in Literature in 1946. His best-known works, including *Steppenwolf* and

Siddhartha, explore the individual's search for spirituality and self-identity. (pp. 114–15)

CARL HILTY (2/28/1833–10/12/1909) was a Swiss philosopher, lawyer, and author who wrote about happiness, the meaning of life and work, developing good habits, and winning the battles of life. (p. 154)

VICTOR HUGO (2/26/1802–5/22/1885) was one of the greatest French writers of poetry, plays, and novels, including *Les Misérables* and *The Hunchback of Notre Dame.* His works often dealt with social injustice and the lives of the poor and were so popular that they influenced French political reform. (pp. 158–59)

HENRIK IBSEN (3/20/1828–5/23/1906) was a Norwegian playwright known as the "father of modern theater." His critical eye and courage to look deeply at contemporary life and accepted morals surprised his audience but made him one of the most distinguished playwrights in Europe. His *A Doll's House*, about a married woman taking control of her own fate, was controversial at the time, but today it is one of the world's most performed plays. (p. 212)

HELEN KELLER (6/27/1880–6/1/1968) was a lecturer, author, and political activist. As a result of a disease when she was just one and a half years old, she became deaf and blind, leaving her unable to communicate. When she was six, her parents found a tutor by the name of Anne Sullivan, who eventually was able to teach Helen how to communicate with her fingers. She learned several forms of communication and became the first blind and deaf person to graduate from college. She became an advocate for people with disabilities, among other causes, and cofounded the American Civil Liberties Union. (pp. 126 and 146)

YOSHIDA KENKO (1284–1350) was a Japanese writer and Buddhist monk who wrote about the beauty of nature, life and death, traditions, friendship, and other worldly and spiritual subjects. The quote comes from his *Essays in Idleness*, one of the most studied works of medieval Japanese literature. (p. 220)

ELLEN KEY (12/11/1849–4/25/1926) was a Swedish writer, educator, and feminist whose ideas on love and marriage and moral conduct had a wide influence. She was an early advocate of a child-centered approach to education. (p. 100)

MARTIN LUTHER KING JR. (1/15/1929–4/4/1968) was a Baptist minister and leader of the American Civil Rights Movement in the 1950s and 1960s. He advocated nonviolence and civil disobedience to promote equal rights for black people in the United States. In 1963, he helped organize the March on Washington, where he gave his famous "I Have a Dream" speech. (pp. 18 and 68)

D. H. LAWRENCE (9/11/1885–3/2/1930) was an English writer and poet, one of the most influential authors of the twentieth century. His *Lady Chatterley's Lover* was banned in the United States and in England until 1960, when a jury decided to allow its publication. The case was considered a turning point in the history of freedom of expression. In his works, he attempted to challenge the constrictive cultural norms of Western culture. (p. 156)

ABRAHAM LINCOLN (2/12/1809–4/15/1865) was the sixteenth president of the United States from 1861 until his assassination in 1865. He led the country through the Civil War when proslavery states seceded from the Union, and he freed all slaves with the Emancipation Proclamation. He is widely considered to be among the greatest of U.S. presidents. (p. 21)

WANGARI MAATHAI (4/1/1940–9/25/2011) was a Kenyan social, environmental, and political activist and founder of the Green Belt Movement, a nongovernmental organization that focuses on the planting of trees. In 2004, she became the first African woman to be awarded the Nobel Peace Prize, which she won for her "contribution to sustainable development, democracy, and peace." (pp. 97 and 105)

JOAQUIM MARIA MACHADO DE ASSIS (6/21/1839–9/29/1908) was a Brazilian novelist, playwright, and short story writer, widely acclaimed as the country's greatest author. He cofounded and was first president of the Brazilian Academy of Letters, an independent nonprofit dedicated to the care of the "national language" (Portuguese) and the promotion of Brazil's literary arts. (p. 140)

TSUNESABURO MAKIGUCHI (6/6/1871–11/18/1944) was a Japanese reformist educator, author, and philosopher who in 1930 cofounded, with Josei Toda, the Soka Gakkai, now an international movement promoting peace, culture, and education. Makiguchi had been an educator who tried to reform the Japanese education system by introducing a more humanistic, student-centered approach. He opposed the corrupt educational system of the time and was forced into early retirement as a result. Later he and Toda were imprisoned for opposing policies of the militarist government. He died in prison of malnutrition at age seventy-three. (p. 180)

NELSON MANDELA (7/18/18–12/5/2013) was an antiapartheid revolutionary in South Africa and the nation's first black head of state from 1994 to 1999. He won the first fully representative democratic election only four years after being released from twenty-seven years in prison for antigovernment activities. He won international acclaim for his work to abolish the racism, inequality, and poverty of apartheid. The quotes are from *Long Walk to Freedom* and *Conversations with Myself.* The one on p. 128 is the moral of a story he cherished. (pp. 11 and 128)

JOSÉ MARTÍ (1/28/1853–5/19/1895) was a Cuban poet, author, professor, and publisher considered a Cuban national hero. The "Apostle of Cuban Independence," he dedicated his life to liberty and independence from Spain through his writings and political activities. (pp. 87, 102, 138–39, and 188)

BENJAMIN ELIJAH MAYS (8/1/1894–3/28/1984) was an American Baptist minister and civil rights leader who mentored many influential activists, such as Martin Luther King Jr. Considered the "intellectual conscience" of the Civil Rights Movement, his work focused on nonviolence and civil resistance, inspired by Gandhi's teachings. (p. 70)

AMADEU THIAGO DE MELLO (3/30/1926–) is one of the most influential and respected poets in Brazil, an icon of Amazonian literature. He is an internationally known intellectual engaged in the struggle for human rights and to guard against the devastation of the Amazon rainforest. (p. 190)

JOHN STUART MILL (5/20/1806–5/7/1873) was a British philosopher and political economist, one of the most influential thinkers in the nineteenth century. He contributed to social and political theory, especially his views on liberty and freedom of speech. He was also one of the first men to advocate for women's rights. (p. 84)

L. M. MONTGOMERY (11/30/1874–4/24/1942) was a Canadian author best known for *Anne of Green Gables*, a classic of children's literature. She wrote several sequels following the ups and downs of Anne's life and her spirit to always maintain hope and find good in others. This quote is from *Anne of Avonlea*. (p. 213)

PABLO NERUDA (7/12/1904–9/23/1973) was a Nobel Prize-winning poet, politician, and diplomat from Chile. His poetry is rich and varied, from passionate love poems, poetry of common everyday objects, and epics celebrating the struggle of the masses to find freedom. (p. 90)

NICHIREN (2/16/1222–10/13/1282) was a Japanese Buddhist reformer who asserted the superiority of the Lotus Sutra, with its concept of universal Buddhahood. He developed the easily accessible practice of chanting Nam-myoho-renge-kyo, a mantra that includes the sutra's title. He taught people to chant it and share it with others so that everyone can attain Buddhahood and bring peace and prosperity to the world. (pp. 3, 10, 22, 42, 56, 63, 65, 85, 93, 103, 104, 108, 116, 124, 129, 164–65, 170, 178, 198–99, 228, and 234)

FRIEDRICH NIETZSCHE (10/15/1844–8/25/1900) was a German philosopher whose ideas on individuality, morality, and the meaning of existence were a major influence on twentieth century philosophy, theology, and art. (p. 27)

FLORENCE NIGHTINGALE (5/12/1820–8/13/1910) was an English social reformer, statistician, and founder of modern nursing.

Until her work during the Crimean War, nursing was not a respected profession. But during that conflict, she and a team of nurses improved conditions at a military hospital through better sanitation, more efficient administration, and individual care of patients. The death rate there dropped by two-thirds, and after the war she was welcomed home as a hero. She wrote numerous works on safe nursing practices, and her pioneering work in statistics is still influential today. (p. 200)

BEN OKRI (3/15/1959–) is an award-winning Nigerian poet and novelist, considered one of Africa's leading writers. Using what's been termed *magical realism*, he conveys the social and political chaos of the country of his birth. He won the esteemed Booker Prize for his 1991 novel *The Famished Road*. (p. 214)

WILLIAM OSLER (7/12/1849–12/29/1919) was a Canadian physician and one of the founding professors of Johns Hopkins Hospital. There he revolutionized the teaching of medicine, being the first to train medical students at the bedside of the patient. (p. 120)

ROSA PARKS (2/4/1913–10/24/2005) was an activist in the Civil Rights Movement in the United States. She is best known for her important role in the Montgomery bus boycott. After a long day at work as a seamstress, she bravely refused to give up her seat on the bus to a white passenger and was arrested. Protests and a boycott followed, which eventually led to nationwide efforts to end racial segregation of public facilities. The quote is from the book *Dear Mrs. Parks: A Dialogue with Today's Youth.* (p. 20)

BLAISE PASCAL (6/19/1623–8/19/1662) was a French mathematician, physicist, inventor, writer, and Catholic theologian. Credited with inventing the mechanical calculator, he also made significant discoveries in mathematics and the physical sciences. He also wrote prolifically on philosophy, including his *Pensées*, considered a masterpiece in theology and French prose. (p. 80)

AUGUSTE RODIN (11/12/1840–11/17/1917) was a French sculptor considered the father of modern sculpture known for his realistic treatment of the human body. Among his best-known works are "The Thinker" and "The Kiss." (p. 14)

ELEANOR ROOSEVELT (10/11/1884–11/7/1962) was the wife of Franklin Delano Roosevelt, the thirty-second U.S. president, and she served as first lady longer than any other woman.

An outspoken advocate for human rights, civil rights, and women's rights, she was often criticized but stayed determined to redefine the role of first lady. When her husband died in office, she was appointed as a delegate to the United Nations and played a key role in drafting the Universal Declaration of Human Rights. (p. 192)

ANTOINE DE SAINT-EXUPÉRY (6/29/1900–7/31/1944) was a French writer and aviator. His novella *The Little Prince* is his best-known work and has been translated into three hundred languages and dialects. He won several literary awards in France and the National Book Award in the United States. Flying for the Free French Air Force, his plane disappeared on a reconnaissance mission during World War II. (p. 94)

GEORGE SAND (7/1/1804–6/8/1876) was the pen name of Amantine Lucile Aurore Dupin, a French novelist, memoirist, and socialist. She was one of the most popular writers in her lifetime, writing passionately against the inequality of men and women in society and in matters of love. (pp. 35 and 193)

SENECA (4 BC–AD 65) was a Roman philosopher, playwright, and advisor to Emperor Nero. As a follower of Stoicism, he focused on the practical question of how to bring this philosophy to bear on living one's life. Hence his writings are among the most readable of all ancient philosophers. (p. 96)

WILLIAM SHAKESPEARE (4/26/1564–4/23/1616) was an English poet and playwright, considered the greatest writer in the English language and the world's greatest dramatist. His plays are studied, performed, and adapted in cultures around the world, making them the most performed plays in the world. The quote is from "As You Like It." (p. 110)

SHAKYAMUNI BUDDHA (563–483 BCE), or Gautama Buddha, was the spiritual leader whose teachings are the foundation of Buddhism. Born a prince, he renounced the secular world to find spiritual enlightenment. After his awakening, he traveled widely to share his wisdom, teaching people how to unleash their own potential and bring peace and happiness to their lives. (p. 232)

RABINDRANATH TAGORE (5/7/1861–8/7/1941) was a Bengali poet, writer, song composer, painter, and the first non-European to win the Nobel Prize in Literature in 1913. He was highly influential in bringing Indian culture to the West and vice versa. (p. 34)

HENRY DAVID THOREAU (7/12/1817–5/6/1862) was a writer and philosopher in the transcendentalist movement. He is best known for his book *Walden,* his reflection on living a simple life in a cabin he built in the woods near Walden Pond. His essay "Civil Disobedience," in which he argues that the individual must follow one's conscience over the dictates of laws, influenced the passive resistance movements of Mahatma Gandhi and Martin Luther King Jr. (p. 26)

JOSEI TODA (2/11/1900–4/2/1958) was a teacher, businessman, peace activist, and cofounder, in 1930, of the Soka Gakkai, now an international Buddhist community dedicated to peace, culture, and education. Jailed by Japan's militarist government during World War II for "thought crimes," Toda was released from prison just before the end of the war and set about to rebuild the organization, which had been decimated. By the time of his death, he and his closest disciple, Daisaku Ikeda, had developed the Soka Gakkai into one of Japan's most influential lay Buddhist associations. Toward the end of his life, Toda advocated a vision of global citizenship and made a historic declaration calling for the abolition of nuclear weapons. (pp. 2, 47, 72–73, and 222)

LEO TOLSTOY (9/9/1828–11/20/1910) was a Russian writer regarded as one of the greatest authors of all time. He was born to an aristocratic family and lived a privileged youth. But after several years in the army, he experienced several spiritual awakenings that led him to espouse leading a simple, even ascetic, life. His writings on nonviolence and pacifism greatly influenced Mahatma Gandhi and Martin Luther King Jr. (p. 92)

VOLTAIRE (11/21/1694–5/30/1778), born François-Marie Arouet, was a French writer of the Enlightenment, famous for his wit and advocacy of freedom of speech, freedom of religion, and the separation of church and state. His satirical plays, poems, novels, and essays often criticized the monarchy and the church, for which he was exiled more than once. (p. 206)

WALT WHITMAN (5/31/1819–3/26/1892) was an American poet, essayist, and journalist. Widely considered one of the country's greatest poets, he celebrated democracy, nature, love, friendship, and the good of the common person. He also supported the Union during the Civil War by volunteering in army hospitals. The quotes are from his poetry collection *Leaves of Grass*, in the poems "Song of the Open Road" and "By Blue Ontario's Shore." (pp. 48–49 and 145)

BETTY WILLIAMS (5/22/1943–) is a corecipient of the Nobel Peace Prize for her work in finding a peaceful resolution to the Northern Ireland conflict in the late twentieth century. She is cofounder, with other female Peace Prize winners, of the Nobel Women's Initiative and lectures widely on peace, education, interfaith understanding, and children's rights. (pp. 36 and 101)

LU XUN (9/25/1881–10/19/1936) was the pen name for Zhou Shuren, a leading figure of modern Chinese literature. As a novelist, essayist, critic, and translator of foreign literature, he spoke out against feudalistic ideology and oppressive government policies, hoping to inspire a change in people's hearts. (pp. 38–39)

EIJI YOSHIKAWA (8/11/1892–9/7/1962) was a Japanese novelist who achieved great renown by retelling classic historical tales in his own modern style, thus generating a renewed interest in the past. Among his best-known works is *Musashi*, an epic novel of the Samurai era in Japan, from which this quote was taken. (p. 181)

MALALA YOUSAFZAI (7/12/1997–) is a Pakistani activist for female education in her native northwest Pakistan, where the Taliban had banned girls from attending school. When she was fifteen, the Taliban attempted to assassinate her for her activism. The attempt sparked international support for her and her movement. In 2014, she became the youngest person to win a Nobel Peace Prize. (p. 171)

STEFAN ZWEIG (11/28/1881–2/22/1942) was an Austrian novelist, playwright, and biographer who during the height of his career was one of the most popular writers in the world. An ardent pacifist, he left Germany after Hitler's rise to power and lived in exile in the United States and Brazil. The quote comes from his memoir, *The World of Yesterday*, completed just before his death. (p. 98)